WAKEFIE

Triggers

Geoff Goodfellow was born in Adelaide in 1949 and began writing poetry in 1983. His three poetry collections, *No Collars No Cuffs*, *Bow Tie & Tails* and *No Ticket No Start*, are used in schools across Australia. Geoff conducts performances and writing workshops in schools, colleges and universities, correctional institutions, on building sites and in corporate boardrooms.

By *the same author*

No Collars No Cuffs
Bow Tie & Tails
No Ticket No Start

Triggers

GEOFF GOODFELLOW

Turning experiences into poetry

WAKEFIELD PRESS

Published by Wakefield Press in association with
the Australian Association for the Teaching of English

Wakefield Press
PO Box 2266
Kent Town
South Australia 5071

First published May 1992 in association with the
Australian Association for the Teaching of English

Copyright © Geoff Goodfellow, 1992

All rights reserved. This book is copyright. Apart from
any fair dealings for the purposes of private study,
research, criticism or review, as permitted under the
Copyright Act, no part may be reproduced without
written permission. Enquiries should be addressed to
the publisher.

Edited by Graham Rowlands
Designed by Ann Wojczuk

Typeset by AdverType
Printed by Hyde Park Press, Adelaide

Cataloguing-in-publication data

Goodfellow, Geoff, 1949-
Triggers.
ISBN 1 86254 276 7.
1. Goodfellow, Geoff, 1949-
– Technique. 2. Poetry –
Authorship. 3. Poetics. I. Title.
808.1

For my daughter
Grace Collette Goodfellow

Author's Note

The author is indebted to Michael Bollen, Stephanie Johnston, Anna Bianchi, Graham Rowlands, Jane Arms, Barbara Hourigan, Caroline Cleland and Jeremy Cogan for their critical advice, energy and enthusiasm during the preparation of *Triggers*.

Preface

To write a poem requires inspiration. It also requires craft. Poets need 'triggers' to set them off, and they need to be able to use words to convey meaning. This book is designed to help out on both fronts. It shows how one poet has been inspired to write by the events of his everyday life and how he has developed methods for turning those events into poems.

Triggers is for writers from young adult upwards. It treats poetry writing as a serious activity, without relying on technical jargon. It combines poems, prose 'yarns' describing the events and social issues that triggered the poems, detailed technical commentary and craft notes, some original drafts of published poems, and what are called 'The Sting', exercises to trigger poems from the reader. The text is written in a lively style that invites the reader to participate both in reading and writing. Geoff Goodfellow explains how he became interested in poetry from an 'ordinary' background and asks his readers to use their 'ordinary' experiences to write their own poems. He argues that poetry is a matter of vision and revision, that although the words rarely come easily, the secret is to make them look as if they do.

He shows how a love bite on a checkout operator's neck, a piece of discarded foil, and an argument about getting out of bed in the morning have triggered poems and sets about making plain some of the techniques of writing poetry: rhyme, punctuation, rhythm, the construction of stanzas, puns, imagery and satire. The reader learns that *nothing* in a poem is there by chance, that there is a purpose to every word, pause and dash.

For Geoff Goodfellow, technique is a means to an end. He calls on readers to reflect on social issues – domestic violence, abuses of power – and to use poetry to express their passions and their concerns.

Contents

1 Triggered to Write 1
2 Triggered by Slang 9
3 Imagery for Imagery's Sake 17
4 Working Images 25
5 Telling Other People's Stories 37
6 Documentaries 49
7 Using Language to Move Mountains 59
8 Rhythm, Rhyme and Sticks and Stones 71
9 Portrait Poems 87
10 Puns 103
11 Researching 113
12 Satire 125

Triggered to Write

GEOFF GOODFELLOW

What sets me off

THE POET

I was always a great yarn spinner at school, but I didn't realise then that I could turn those spoken yarns into written poems. I left school at fifteen after failing to gain my Intermediate Certificate (the year ten equivalent). I was brought up in a working-class, inner northern suburb Adelaide home with a mother and father, an elder sister, and two younger brothers. We never starved or went hungry, but we never pulled the heads off too many king prawns. I went to a convent for my first three years before swapping to a state school. I was a fairly lazy student, not dumb, but I always seemed to be at ease with spoken language, probably because we talked so much at home. Dad was a salesman and the spoken word was his wage-packet. Mum ran the household. She was skilled in her use of words, seldom being beaten by a crossword puzzle. If any of us used incorrect grammar or pronunciation, she'd pull us up. In their ways they both fostered my ability with language. The TV set would go off each evening when we'd eat dinner and we'd be encouraged to express our views about events of the day. Very early on, I learned about the power of language to influence decisions as I negotiated variations on bed-time and who was going to wash the dishes. As far as I can remember, my parents never censored a subject.

I started work as a butcher a couple of days after clearing out my locker. But I was attracted by the lure of big money from the high-risk jobs that were so readily available and I quickly moved through a succession of them. I worked as a steel-fixer, concrete sprayer, oil rig worker, truck driver, labourer and salesman before settling down as a self-employed carpenter.

In 1982, the effects of nearly twenty years of strenuous manual work caught up with me. I finished up in traction in hospital with a specialist telling me that I had two compressed discs in my lower back and that an operation was inevitable. I wouldn't accept his opinion and signed myself out of hospital, choosing instead to go home and crawl around on my hands and knees. I spent eighteen months, my body racked with pain, as I sought out chiropractors, physiotherapists, acupuncturists, even an old Polish man in a backyard garage. I must have seen twenty different people before I found a physiotherapist who was able to straighten my back and ease my pain. It was while this man was treating me that I started to write.

I'd never been a reader of anything but newspapers and magazines since leaving school, but after twelve months on all fours at home and having exhausted everyone's telephone number in my personal directory, I crawled across a book that had been left lying on the floor by my eldest son. My first thought was to put it down again. I can remember thinking, I'm too tough to read poetry – the book was the *Selected Works of Banjo Patterson* – but when I started to read it, I couldn't put it down. I was an immediate convert. After reading it from cover to cover, I began to wonder if I could write like that myself.

My first attempts were clumsy, but that didn't stop me because at the time I thought they were good. I soon became curious about what other people might have been saying, became a reader and consumed the contents of dozens of books. I could soon see the value of other styles and recognise some of the techniques, but there didn't seem to be just one right way.

As I became more mobile, I started attending Adelaide's Friendly Street Poetry readings, buying more books, listening to other poets, and seeking the advice and feedback of poets whose work I admired. In September of 1983 I had my first poem published in a little literary magazine called *Ash*. My career was launched.

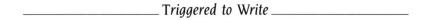

Triggered to Write

THE POET

I realised that to be able to capture the events around me on the page and in performance, I needed to find a way to transcribe the everyday language that surrounded me. The rhythms of people's speech and their quirks of language are revealing of their characters and their social situations – what they are trying to do, and what they are up against.

I felt threatened by the notion that a poet needed to have a style. For a time I tried to write in rhyming verse with a regular beat but found that it limited my capacity to tell stories. And I wanted to do just that – to tell stories in poems in my everyday language and allow the characters in my poems to speak in their own voices. I soon learnt that I was up against two of my old stumbling blocks – grammar and punctuation – but I needed them as vital allies.

The only formal punctuation I use without exception is at the end of a poem. You'll always find a full stop used to signify that I have no more to offer on the subject. In between you will find my MPD (measured punctuation device), arrived at by hitting the space bar on the keyboard three times. It can be interpreted as a three-second delay, which allows for a simpler reading than installing commas, full stops, and so on. I complete the poem's punctuation by complementing those three-second signals with the occasional dash (to instruct the reader to pause for a moment to consider what they have just read) or with three full stops in succession (to show my readers that I want them to let their minds travel much further). Those markings are all determined by the rhythms of speech. I want my poems not just to flow, but to communicate. While writing a poem, I continually read it aloud to get an accurate sense that the rhythm of the poem corresponds with a real voice pattern. I can recognise where a breath may need to be drawn – tap/tap/tap on the space bar; where a natural pause may occur – tap/tap/tap; where tension has built to the point that it must be shown – tap/tap/tap; where the contents of a line need to be considered for a moment – tap/tap/tap. Those taps determine if the poem is having an impact.

_____ *Triggered to Write* _____

THE POET

An important part of fine-tuning a poem is finding the right length for the line. I try to work the line length to seek some type of response from the line which will follow. Here is the opening stanza of 'Beware of The Penguins'.

> 'the first school for me
>   was one that made young
> boys   into little men
>   (till grade four)
> & young girls
>   into little ladies
> with straw hats'

The opening line puts the reader in a particular landscape: 'school'. It lets the reader know that this will be a poem about 'me' as a little boy at school. What is important about that school, you might ask. You could try to find an answer on the next line from 'was one that made young'. But that doesn't make sense. You can't work it out until you ask, 'Into what?' 'Into little men' is the answer. There is a long gap then between 'boys' and the next phrase on the same line. But there is a long time until 'young boys' turn 'into little men'. I haven't used an enormous gap or gone to another line to separate the two because, as you find out on the next line, it's only '(till grade four)' that we're talking about. I've used brackets on that phrase to treat it as more of an aside. The poem then moves away from boys and in the next line swings into '& young girls'. So what did the school make those young girls into? Answer: 'into little ladies'. But how did it do that?: 'with straw hats'. Can you really make a young girl into a little lady by putting a straw hat on her head? The poem is supposed to make you think about questions, not give you answers.

Part of my fine-tuning relies on dividing the poem into stanzas. With stanzas I can separate speakers in the poem from the poem's narrator or from other speakers, or I can highlight a point. Stanzas also give me an opportunity to take a leap in

Triggered to Write

THE POET

time, or to change voice to escape from telling everything in detail, point after consecutive point. Poetry is more suited to understatement than overstatement, and it's the writer's job to determine the balance. Each word in a poem must have particular values, must convey not only meaning but mood. The essence of poetry for me is to compress the language to its most economical form. For this reason I like to use words with double meanings. This can heighten the intensity of the poem or allow me to bounce off a word and move the poem in another direction without losing coherence.

I set out to write poems that work either on or off the page. I understand poetry to be a tool of communication. The oral tradition of performance poetry is particularly suited to the nineties because these days so many of our communications systems are audio-visual.

An enormous amount of imagery conveyed to us by TV, video and film originates from the United States. In 1988 I gave my first overseas reading at the Seattle Pacific University. It was a one-hour session attended by about forty people. Judging from the response, I thought the audience had enjoyed the poems. When I called for questions, however, I was greeted by silence. I suppose I was suprised. After a lengthy pause, an expatriate Australian stood up and said, 'Hey man, you know why there's been no questions? You've been talking Australian, man, not English.' Once the ice was broken, the questions started to flow. They were fascinated by the Australian slang in my poems and were soon pointing out to me their equivalents. I now recognise my Australian storehouse of language: it has come most noticeably from my father, who passed on to me the words and phrases that his father brought back from the first world war and that he added to during service in the second. One of my brothers was a merchant seaman with a colourful language of rhyming slang and unusual turns of phrase. Another was a lightweight boxing champion. Through my work in gaols, youth centres, rehabilitation centres and refuges, I've been exposed to much new language.

Triggered to Write

THE POET

When I went to high school in the sixties you could bet that the poems I had to study had been written by members of the Dead Poets' Society: poets who had lived in Britain or the United States and knew nothing about Australia, poets who had lived in another era, used another language, and were as likely to come into the classroom as Elvis.

Triggered to Write

Triggered by Slang

'SHRAPNEL'

Using language as loose change

THE TRIGGER

Shrapnel is the metal fragments of exploding bombs. It wounds or kills you if it hits you. Even a piece that has travelled a huge distance and lost its velocity can cause severe bruising.

For as long as I remember, I've used the word 'shrapnel' as slang for 'loose change', as has the rest of my family.

At a supermarket checkout one afternoon I used the term in conversation with the cash register operator. The term didn't register with her. While I was explaining what I meant I noticed a huge love bite on her neck. For a moment I contemplated teasing her, but I was as polite as she was. I observed etiquette. As I walked home, however, I wondered whether she'd been wounded in love or had had a victory.

How could I show that scene in the shop in a poem? Look for the changes between one of my drafts of 'Shrapnel' and the final version of the poem.

Triggered by Slang

THE DRAFT

Shrapnel

That'll be $2.47   she says
with a ring to her voice
     & i dug into my sky rocket
hang on   i said
     i'll give y' my shrapnel

& she looked at me vaguely
     queriously –
from eyes as washed out
as her summer blue uniform
     a different uniform
to the past eleven years

& while she looks at me
     the same way she'd probably
looked at her science teacher
     a love bite as large
as a new born fist slides up
     above her collar

Triggered by Slang

THE POEM

Shrapnel

That'll be $2.47 she said
   with a ring to her voice

hang on i said
digging into my sky rocket
   i'll give y' my shrapnel

& she looked at me
   vaguely
querulously
from eyes as washed out
as a summer blue uniform
   a different uniform
from her past eleven years

& while she looked at me ...
the same way she'd probably
looked at her science teacher –
   a love bite as large
as a new born fist
   slid up above her collar

thank you sir she said

thank you miss i said.

Triggered by Slang

Shrapnel

That'll be $2.47 she said   I changed the tense
    with a ring to her voice

hang on i said   slang for 'pocket'
    digging into my sky rocket
    i'll give y' my shrapnel

got the spelling right at last!

& she looked at me
     vaguely
querulously
from eyes as washed out
as a summer blue uniform
    a different uniform
from her past eleven years

& while she looked at me ...
the same way she'd probably
looked at her science teacher –
    a love bite as large
    as a new born fist
       slid up above her collar

I always use italics to show when a character in the poem is speaking

thank you sir she said
thank you miss i said.

———— Triggered by Slang ————

THE STING

People use slang all the time. A posh word for slang is 'idiom'. 'Posh' is a slang word itself, so you can see how easily we slip into slang words. 'Slip into' is a kind of slang, but would more likely be called 'colloquial', or 'everyday' speech, the way we all talk most of the time.

The Macquarie Dictionary defines slang as language that differs from standard or written speech in vocabulary and construction, involving humour, ellipsis, and metaphor. It is less conservative and more informal than standard speech, and is sometimes regarded as being in some way inferior; it may be vulgar or abusive language; it may be the jargon of a particular class or profession.

Some slang stays around year after year, but there are also fashions in slang. School students use slang words that your parents have never heard of and hardly understand, and probably some that they choose not to understand! Your ordinary everyday speech is a mixture of the colloquial, the formal, modern slang and traditional slang. Make a list of what you regard as your most commonly used, colourful slang phrases then have a go (slang!) at using some of them in a poem.

Triggered by Slang

Imagery for Imagery's Sake

'A HAPPY BALANCE'

Don't tell, show

THE TRIGGER

'A Happy Balance' is a poem that uses imagery for imagery's sake. Well, almost. As it sits on the page, it is, but when I was writing the poem, it was more. But I can't always just write to make a point. Sometimes I have to leave the meaning open for my readers or listeners, or both, to sort out.

I'll give you a hint, though, of what triggered this poem.

I was conducting a series of writing workshops with young teenage girls who'd been sexually, physically and emotionally abused. Before heading off to meet them again, I was sitting in an office up a flight of stairs looking out over a courtyard fronting a child care centre. I was gazing out of the window dreamily when a young girl and her mother walked out. I was attracted by the innocent trust the youngster placed in her mother. After anonymously observing them disappear from my view, I knew I'd been provided with the balance to negotiate the day. Sometimes an image can be enough.

THE DRAFT

A Happy Balance

All of 3 years old
holding mummy's hand
   she pranced along
a concrete ledge
   shoebox sized –
in bright red shoes
   pigtails bobbing
with every bounce
   a balanced arrangement

until midway –
she hung out like
an outrigger

still young enough
to give full trust

& lucky enough
   to laugh.

―――― Imagery for Imagery's Sake ――――

THE POEM

A Happy Balance

All of three years old
holding mummy's hand
   she pranced along
a stretched out shoebox
ledge of concrete
   bringing down
her bright red shoes
& frilly socks
   while ribboned pig-tails
bobbed
   at every bounce

a happy balance

till midway
   she swung out like
an outrigger

still young enough
   to give full trust

& lucky enough
   to laugh.

Imagery for Imagery's Sake

THE CRAFT

'A Happy Balance' went through seven drafts. In my first draft I'd written:

> 'she walked along
> a shoebox
> sized concrete ledge'

but that was prose. I was telling it. I had to *show* it! I changed it in the second draft to:

> 'she pranced along'

That word showed the action. By the third draft I'd added two more words and rearranged the next two lines:

> 'a stretched out shoebox
> ledge of concrete'

Back on my first draft I'd written:

> 'hanging out like
> an outrigger'

But 'hanging out' sounded like words that belonged in a drug poem. I changed it to:

> '   she swung out like
> an outrigger'

I wanted to get the phrasing right, to keep that motion and action. In draft three I'd written:

> '& pig-tails bobbed
> with every bounce'

Notice the action is still evident with that 'bounce'. But you can't have pig-tails without securing them somehow. I wanted to give this young child all the credit possible for her appearance. So I included more imagery:

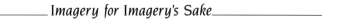
Imagery for Imagery's Sake

THE CRAFT

> ' while ribboned pig-tails
> bobbed
> at every bounce'

Now that central line 'a happy balance' didn't come easily. It didn't appear until the seventh and final draft. It had started off as:

> 'a balanced arrangement'

and stayed that way until draft five when it became:

> 'a very balanced arrangement'

But in draft seven it simply became 'a happy balance', using her image and perhaps a bit more. I was able to use the line for my poem's title.

THE STING

Think of another kind of happy balance, perhaps from nature or art (for example, the Mona Lisa's smile), architecture (for example, the symmetrical nature of many buildings), sport (for example, physical balance or the balance of scores) or some human activity (for example, a baby's first steps). Make a list of some images that come to mind when you think of balance and extend the ideas they bring to mind by drafting a poem.

Imagery for Imagery's Sake

Working Images

'BEWARE OF THE PENGUINS'

Tell by showing

THE TRIGGER

When I wrote 'Beware of The Penguins' in 1983, I was living in Claxton Street in the west end of Adelaide. I was driving an unusual vehicle at that time, a D1510 dual-cab International truck. It was an ex-Telecom vehicle, extremely ugly, with big lumpy seventeen inch dual wheels. One morning I went out to fire up the truck and noticed that one of the rear tyres was flat. I'd owned the beast for around six months but hadn't had to lift a spanner to it. I cursed a bit, but at least I was prepared. I had a hydraulic jack, a wheel-brace, and a spare tyre. All I needed was energy. As it was a warm summer morning, I cancelled the doctor's appointment I'd made, deciding instead to take up the task at my leisure, settling for a cup of coffee to allow me to contemplate the job.

After spending about thirty minutes trying to 'crack' the wheel nuts, I began to feel frustrated. I thought I'd done everything properly. I'd used the principles of leverage that my science teacher had taught me at Nailsworth Tech, and I'd still had no luck. I was determined, however, and persevered. I was using the strength in my right arm, using the same hand that I wrote with, the same hand I'd used to swing a hammer and a saw in the previous ten years when I'd worked on various building sites. I was balanced correctly but, swing as I might, I couldn't budge any of those nuts. By this time I'd ripped off my T-shirt and was just wearing shorts and thongs. My arm had begun to ache so I decided to take a breather, go inside out of the heat, sip a cold drink, and come back with renewed vigour. Ten minutes later I returned, selected a wheel nut, and put the

THE TRIGGER

socket over it, but at the last moment I changed my mind and position, and decided to tackle it with my left. I swung on the bar, then 'crack'. The ease surprised me. I can remember thinking, I've still got four to go ... I must have chosen the easy one. I continued with my left arm. It was just a matter of 'crack', 'crack', 'crack', 'crack'. I was so astounded that I walked back into the house, the task unfinished, shaking my head. I went into the bathroom and stood in front of the large wall mirror, staring at the profile of my neck and shoulders. Without being aware of what I was doing I flexed the muscles in the trunk of my body, noticing immediately that the muscle definition on the left was far greater than that of the right. Why? I had always used my right hand as my leading hand ... or so I thought.

I sat at the kitchen table, under no pressure to finish the job, feeling confused. I closed my eyes and allowed my mind to wander. The years clicked away like notches on a ratchet bar until once again I could see myself as a young boy, a grade-one student at Our Lady of the Sacred Heart College at Enfield. With my eyes closed and my head cradled in my hands I could see myself being harassed and tormented by a pink face set in a white band, the body in a flowing black shroud. I was being taught not to write with my left hand, the heavy leather strap turning my left hand as red as my blue eyes. But as the cruelty of those times resurfaced, the more pleasurable moments came too. I remembered the summer mornings under the gum trees, the dappled light shading out the fierce sun as we sang our times tables, the rhythms that still run through me when I multiply sums now. Most of all I remember the constant worry of being left-handed or different.

I dredged up the ending for 'Beware of The Penguins' by thinking back to the day I took two of my young sons to the zoo. They were keen to see the penguins receive their afternoon feed. Although I tried to watch it with them, I had to walk away and stand alone, accept their curiosity and watch over them from a distance. I had seen far too many penguins in my childhood.

Working Images

THE POEM

Beware of The Penguins

the first school for me
   was one that made young
boys   into little men
   (till grade four)
& young girls
   into little ladies
with straw hats

school was uplifting for me
with Sister Mary what's-her-name
   lifting me of the boards
by my left ear   arms
   flailing like a windmill

& she did

until that parent/teacher day
   in the quadrangle
& i said
      do it now
      do it now

i often remember
that protesting penguin
with the red face   & it wasn't
hot flushes that day

in summer   classes
under the gums singing
multiplication songs
   even fourteen times
tables   & i still sing them
   but now
on the bathroom scales
   where everything is changing

THE POEM

sitting at that flip
top desk   eastern side
of the class for the morning sun
   in prickly grey melange

she'd eyeball me

then beat that short
thick heavy leather strap
into her palm & tell me
   don't write left-handed
OR ELSE!
   *sick people silly people
crazy people in hospitals
write left-handed!*

& i worried

& changed

then beat all-comers in the
left-handed arm wrestles
   & i worried
if i could still go crazy

& i saw the girl
who sucked her thumb
in grade three
   crawl around the classroom
on all fours
   dummy in mouth

& i saw the girl
who dribbled regularly
on her desk top   get her nose
rubbed in it
   & i can still see
snail trails
   shining off her desk top
on my way to recess

THE POEM

a sixpenny cream bun
   icing sugar
smothering my freckles
   dandruff
down my Silver Fleece Jumper

& i still love
strawberry jam

but when i go to the zoo
now
   i usually give
the penguins
   a miss.

Beware of The Penguins

I was seeing this poem: there are a million things in any poem, but this one is strongly visual

    the first school for me
     was one that made young
    boys into little men
     (till grade four)
    & young girls   *— they'd need more than*
     into little ladies *straw hats, wouldn't they?*
    with straw hats

a pun – look at me – up school was ⟨uplifting⟩ for me
I go   with Sister Mary what's-her-name
     ⟨lifting⟩ me off the boards
    by my left ear arms
     flailing like a windmill

    & she did

    until that parent/teacher day
     in the quadrangle
    & i said
      do it now
      do it now   *all the nuns were penguins*
    i often remember *– (a metaphor)*
    that protesting penguin
    with the red face & it wasn't
    hot flushes that day

    in summer classes ← *classes, social classes*
    under the gums singing
    multiplication songs
     even fourteen times
    tables & i still sing them
     but now
      on the bathroom scales
my weight, metric where everything is changing
conversion

BETWEEN THE LINES

it was better outside sitting at that flip
top desk   eastern side
of the class for the morning sun
   in prickly grey melange

she'd eyeball me ← *she didn't just look at me*

then beat that short
thick heavy leather strap
into her palm & tell me
   don't write left-handed
OR ELSE!
   sick people silly people
crazy people in hospitals
write left-handed!

& i worried

& changed

then beat all-comers in the
left-handed arm wrestles   *wrestling her and others*
   & i worried   *in the playground*
if i could still go crazy

& i saw the girl
who sucked her thumb
in grade three
   crawl around the classroom
on all fours
   dummy in mouth

& i saw the girl
who dribbled regularly   *I wasn't the only one*
on her desk top   get her nose
rubbed in it
   & i can still see
snail trails
   shining off her desk top
on my way to recess

_____ Working Images _____

BETWEEN THE LINES

there I was   a sixpenny cream bun
                      icing sugar
                      smothering my freckles
                           dandruff
                      down my Silver Fleece jumper

                      & i still love
                      strawberry jam

                      but when i go to the zoo
                      now
                         i usually give   *punch it home: well,*
                         the penguins   *I didn't write it because*
                           a miss.   *I liked the old girl, did I?*

Working Images

THE STING

Your school experiences are different from mine, but they can trigger a poem. It'll take more than one go to get it right. Here's a way to start working. Look closely at 'Beware of the Penguins' and you'll see that I put it together by using a series of visual images from my memories of early days at school. I've written down some of them underneath.

> 'little ladies with straw hats'
>
> 'Sister Mary what's-her-name
>   lifting me off the boards
> by my left ear'
>
> '(my) arms flailing like a windmill'
>
> 'that protesting penguin
> with the red face'

Find some more visual images from my poem and write them down. You could start to write your own poem by trying to visualise your early school days. What images strike you? If you start to see a confusing blur of pictures, try to focus on a particular day – your first day at high school, for example. Were you excited to be joining 'the big kids'? Or focus on an event such as sports day, a new game or a hero's visit.

I hope you've got the picture, or a list of little pictures, 'snaps' from your past. Now it's your job to shuffle them about, discard some, prune some, add more as you go along and put in linking words so you have a poem that shows your reader something about your early school days, and how you feel about them. If you like, you can steal my first line: 'the first school for me'.

5
Telling Other People's Stories

'WHAT CHANCE HAS A BLOKE GOT'

*To tell other people's stories,
you have to really listen to them*

THE TRIGGER

I was conducting a writing workshop in the maximum security division of Adelaide's Yatala Labour Prison one Tuesday evening in 1985, when one of the volunteer participants, a young fellow serving a life sentence, started asking me questions about various people we knew in common. He had been locked up for about ten years but had known me for twenty years through my association with his father. He was full of questions. We had talked about quite a few different people when he stumbled across the name of an older bloke we both knew very well. Now this bloke is very colourful. His language, mannerisms, outlook on life, all seem to reflect an Australia of an earlier era. We found ourselves talking about the Rabbit Man, a mighty character who earned a living selling bunnies in the pubs of Adelaide. Many people survived in the Depression by selling rabbits in pubs, but this bloke was still managing to pull off the same rort fifty years later. I told him that nothing much had changed. The Rabbit Man was still wearing stovepipe trousers and slapping Brylcream on his hair, still the same larrikin he'd always been. I'd often bump into him in the saloon bar of a particular pub on a Friday night and I promised to pass on best wishes. On the following Friday night I was bracing the bar around seven o'clock when in comes the Rabbit Man – red-faced, bleary-eyed and sporting a cheeky grin. I launched into how I'd run into the young fellow, gave him a bit of a run-down and did as I had promised. The Rabbit Man is one hundred per cent staunch and made me promise, 'Scouts' Honour', to reciprocate the young fellow's greeting. I did, but messed up the first time, putting up

THE TRIGGER

the wrong hand. He's a cagey old bloke, picked me up on it straight off and made me do it right.

Soon after I had put my left hand up, he began to look a bit agitated. He leaned in towards me to exclude others nearby and explained that he wanted a bit of advice. He'd been brought up in the old school. What he was about to tell me, in his dry, laconic style, told me more about himself and his view of women than about anything else.

THE POEM

What Chance Has A Bloke Got

listen he says
you've heard i've lost me cook
haven't y'

yeah   i've heard
a bit of a whisper

well   can i buy y' one
& get in y'r ear
she's got me stumped
    dead set

he's backed me into a corner
& said   25 bloody years
& she lobs this on me
    no other bloke
just this bloody women's
liberation bullshit
    wants to be on her own

i've told her
    if there's a mug   you're off
& if i know him   he's off too
    but no   no mug   just muggins me
i mean look at me
    five foot nothing
a fat ex-jockey who can skin rabbits
& rock'n'roll
    what chance has a bloke got

she's moved into a flat
on her pat malone
    left me on the farm with
me 2 lads   the horses
& the dogs

―――― Telling Other People's Stories ――――

THE POEM

*i've worked me guts out
all me life
   2 jobs plus breaking horses
on the weekends
   even chucked a leg
over a few windowsills
when things got really desperate
   she's never had to ask f'r
a thing   not a bloody thing*

*told her to get home f'r
lunch Mother's Day
   & she come too –
we're in the kitchen
by the back door
& i says to her
   y' see that Palomino colt
out there
   she says 'yeah'
& i said   that's mine*

*& i says y' see that
blue heeler pup over there
   she says 'yeah'
& i said   that's mine*

*& i says now get over there
& look in that bloody mirror
'cos that's mine too
   you're going nowhere*

*& she's up & hoofed it
   women   y' just can't work
'em out   i've given her everything
   given her the bloody lot*

yeah   i said   you sure have.

Telling Other People's Stories

THE CRAFT

Poems in which I reproduce yarns that people tell me ('dramatic monologues') don't normally take on massive changes in the drafts. I listen carefully to people's stories and I'm able to repeat them on the page pretty much as I hear them. In writing these poems I spend most of my time pruning and shaping someone's original words so that they work for me: they make the point I want to make about the person who is talking.

In my first draft of this poem, the fourth stanza started:

> 'well   we backed away
> into a corner'

In a later version it became:

> 'he's backed me into a corner'

but only after I tried reading the poem aloud, aping the movements we'd made in that bar. He did 'back me into a corner', but it didn't have much to do with my wishes that we moved there. It was his story. He was going to give it to me, coming, ready or not.

Further on in the poem, I had written in the first draft:

> *'i mean look at me*
> *five foot nothing*
> *& all i can do is skin rabbits*
> *& rock 'n' roll*
> *what chance have i got'*

I realised when I reworked it that I hadn't shown enough of the Rabbit Man. My readers knew he was short, but they didn't know he was overweight, so I dropped '& all i can do is' and replaced it with 'a fat ex-jockey who can'. The effect was to create a much stronger character, someone I believe you can start to see.

I also changed 'what chance have i got' to 'what chance has a bloke got'. In this stanza the Rabbit Man describes himself in a self-pitying way to try to win my sympathy. By calling himself 'a bloke', rather than 'I', he is pushing the boat out, trying to win

THE CRAFT

me over, as if he's saying, 'I'm a bloke, you're a bloke, you'll understand.' In the same way as he physically backed me into a corner, he used words to manoeuvre me. But if you compare the words he used to describe his wife (such as 'me cook'), you'll see why he didn't eventually win either my sympathy or the reader's.

Until my fifth draft, the sixth stanza read:

> '& i'm home on the farm
> with me 2 lads the horses
> & the dogs'

It didn't convey strongly enough his self-pitying tone. So I changed it to:

> '   left me on the farm with
> me 2 lads   the horses
> & the dogs'

In the next stanza, the line 'when things got really desperate' is how the final version appears. But, 'really' was added only during draft four. It helps the rhythm and adds desperation to his tone of voice. That line was originally followed by 'she's never wanted for anything'. That's where the stanza finished in my second draft. But, in the third draft, I changed the line to 'she's never had to ask fer anything' to end the stanza. In draft four I changed it to 'she's never had to ask for a thing'. In the fifth draft I hit upon:

> '   she's never had to ask fer
> a thing   not a bloody thing'

Read that aloud and you'll see how the extra four words add to the Rabbit Man's 'voice' as he belts home his point. As a final bit of fine-tuning I changed 'fer' to 'f'r', which seemed a better way to write the same sound. Poetry is about sound. You have to make the music ring in the words or the words ring with your music. It usually takes many drafts to find that magic. It isn't easy, but the trick is to make it look easy.

Telling Other People's Stories

BETWEEN THE LINES

What Chance Has A Bloke Got

scene setting   listen he says
you've heard i've lost me cook   *he's a male chauvinist*
haven't y'

yeah   i've heard
a bit of a whisper

well   can i buy y' one   *slang, idiom,*
& get in y'r ear   *colloquialisms: you know*
she's got me stumped   *what they are*
   dead set

he's backed me into a corner
& said   25 bloody years
& she lobs this on me
   no other bloke
just this bloody women's
liberation bullshit
   wants to be on her own

i've told her
   if there's a mug   you're off
& if i know him   he's off too   *another colloquialism*
   but no   no mug   just mugging me
i mean look at me
   five foot nothing
a fat ex-jockey who can skin rabbits
& rock'n'roll
   what chance has a bloke got

she's moved into a flat
on her pat malone   *her own*
   left me on the farm with
me 2 lads   the horses
& the dogs

Telling Other People's Stories

BETWEEN THE LINES

> i've worked me guts out
> all me life
>   2 jobs plus breaking horses
> on the weekends
>   even chucked a leg
> over a few windowsills   *crime*
> when things got really desperate
>   she's never had to ask f'r
> a thing   not a bloody thing
>
> told her to get home f'r
> lunch Mother's Day
>   & she come too –
> we're in the kitchen
> by the back door
> & i says to her
>   y' see that Palomino colt
> out there
>   she says 'yeah'
> & i said   that's mine
>
> & i says y' see that
> blue heeler pup over there
>   she says 'yeah'
> & i said   that's mine
>
> & i says now get over there
> & look in that bloody mirror
> 'cos that's mine too
>   you're going nowhere
>
> & she's up & hoofed it   *animal status*
>   women   y' just can't work
> 'em out   i've given her everything
>   given her the bloody lot
> yeah   i said   you sure have.

his speech patterns – like everything else he says

it's been his story, but it's also mine – when I've told it: I see through him and you'll see through him. The more colourfully he tells his story, the worse it is for him – in terms of trying to convince his listeners. I make it clear that I don't agree with him.

──────── Telling Other People's Stories ────────

THE STING

Does 'What Chance Has A Bloke Got', or the story, trigger anything for you? You probably know at least one colourful character, someone who loves spinning stories and demands that you listen to them. Maybe it's the person you sit next to on the way to school or the oldie who demands your seat on the bus or train. Perhaps you have a cheeky aunt, a weird neighbour, a grandfather you refer to as 'Captain Havachat' or a brother you call 'Demo' because he demolishes everything in his path. Whoever it is, write down a story you've heard someone tell as if this person is telling it to you. Really think about their typical turns of phrase.

Now you need to shape the story into a poem. You mightn't agree with the story you listen to. Try to show that by letting the person's story speak for itself.

Telling Other People's Stories

Documentaries

'WATCHING'

We change with the times

THE TRIGGER

I had three sons aged fifteen, thirteen and eight when I wrote this poem late in 1984. It was the first week of the Christmas school holidays. While my sons had finished their school work for the year, I was still writing my final essay for presentation at the college I was attending.

I had a spread of reference books in front of me and scraps of note paper containing scribbled facts, sheets of lecture notes, handouts covered with doodles from a semester of boring lectures and an A4 lined pad that I was desperately trying to fill. We were living in a small renovated workers' cottage in the city and no one had a private area to call their own. The cottage had a large family room that had been attached to the rear, but it adjoined the kitchen and formed an open-space living area. It was one of those hot, dry days in which it seems that a trip to the fridge every fifteen minutes is necessary if life is to go on. The fridge stood at one end of the room and the TV set at the other. I was stuck in the middle with my elbows leaning on the kitchen table. The TV was blaring away with cartoons and the fridge was constantly under attack as I sat at the table trying to concentrate. *Trying* certainly seemed to be the word for it.

After about two hours of bedlam the two older boys asked if I'd mind if they went for a walk into Rundle Mall. I was delighted, of course, but asked why, feigning curiosity. They reckoned there'd be a lot of girls in town and they would try to find a couple who looked lonely. It seemed a good enough reason to me. I parted with a bit of spending money so they wouldn't have their style cramped, giving them instructions to be home by

THE TRIGGER

mid-afternoon. Peace at last, I thought, but then I had to spend the next fifteen minutes pacifying Paul, the youngest, trying to explain why it wasn't appropriate for him to go with them. He calmed down eventually and went back to the TV set, squatting on his haunches about one metre from the screen, Inspector Gadget commanding his full attention.

I looked towards him about fifteen minutes later and it appeared he had crept even closer. In a crude attempt to reposition him, I asked him to tell me the time (even though I was wearing a watch). I sat there fascinated, watching him as he moved across the room, sideways like a crab, not allowing his eyes to lose the images on the screen. It was only when he'd travelled the four metres or so required to align himself with the clock that he glanced away and announced the time to be 10:42. He repeated his crab walk in reverse without bumping into a single piece of furniture. When he settled on the floor I had to ask him to back away from the screen. When I was satisfied that he was a safe distance away, I put my head down and continued to write, trying to block out the blare of the box.

When I looked up about thirty minutes later, he was breathing on the screen again. I'd started to tire by then. My neck and shoulders were aching, my back needed a stretch and a channel had started to develop in my third finger from pressing on the pen. The heat inside the house had started to build up too. I thought it would be a good idea for both of us to get out and go for a walk. When I put the idea to Paul, he was up like a rocket, down the long hallway, waiting for me at the front door, yelling out for me to 'hurry up'.

As we walked along Gouger Street he asked me questions like, 'When you were a kid and you had black and white telly, did you still have Inspector Gadget?' 'No,' I replied, shaking my head.

'Well, when you were a kid and you had black and white telly, was everything else black and white?'

'What exactly do you mean?' I asked, raising my eyebrows.

'You know, were buildings and cars and clothes and stuff all black and white, or did you have colours then?'

Documentaries

THE TRIGGER

As we turned into Victoria Square I thought I had found an answer. Pointing to the Post Office clock up in the tower, I asked him to tell me the time. He was looking, but he wasn't answering. I asked again. Still no answer. 'Come on,' I said, 'the clock's up there, tell me the time.'

He shrugged his shoulders and said, 'I dunno.'

'You told me the time at home this morning,' I said.

He looked up and said innocently, 'It's digital.'

I just about fell in the fountain. 'They teach you how to tell the time at school though, don't they?'

'Not at my school,' he said, screwing up his nose.

'What do they teach you at school then?' I asked. 'Aw, computers. We learn computers just about every day, plus we can play games on them some lunch-times when it's wet.'

As we continued walking I was giving some thought to the dilemma of my son growing up not knowing how to tell the time in the traditional way. 'I'll tell you what I think we should do,' I said. 'How about we go up to Edments Jewellers in Rundle Mall and buy a Mickey Mouse watch with hands so I can teach you how to tell the time the old-fashioned way?' He was rapt in the idea and we continued on, hand-in-hand along King William Street, dodging prams and hand-carts and the mid-day rush of office workers who were coming out of the glass towers to bite the end off a pasty or whatever. We travelled in silence, having agreed that he should count the number of people he could see wearing digital watches and I should count the number wearing analogue watches. From the Town Hall to Edments my tally was only a twentieth of Paul's. I had worn an analogue continually for at least twenty years and was suprised to learn that I belonged to a minority. But when I considered the reasons, it began to make sense. Anyone could buy a digital watch for under two dollars or get one free when having a roll of film processed. When I went to school, wearing a watch was a status symbol. Now you could buy a watch with the refund from a handful of empty cool drink bottles.

When we got into Edments, the sales assistant who ap-

Documentaries

proached us was a young girl, perhaps no older than my eldest son. When I told her that we were looking for a Mickey Mouse watch, she looked at me as though I was a day patient on an outing from a psychiatric hospital. A few minutes passed before a young man in a crisp white shirt approached us. I explained myself again and was told that it had been some years since they'd carried that stock. 'I'll show you what all the kids are wearing today,' he said, winking at me. After ducking down behind the counter, he re-appeared with a big box-full of digital watches, the faces containing images of the 'Star Wars' villain, Darth Vader.

I explained that I wanted an analogue, a proper watch, one with hands so I could teach my young son how to tell the time in the traditional way.

'I've got just the thing for you,' he said, pointing a finger towards the ceiling, 'just hold on a tick.' A minute later he handed me a plain-looking chrome watch with a white face and a leather band. It had large, clear numerals and seemed to be ideal. 'It's a bit more expensive,' he said quietly, 'but it's got a Swiss movement and it will last him for years. Fifty-nine dollars.'

'We'll give it a miss,' I said, thanking him, thinking of Laurie Tredrea's pawn shop at the Central Market, knowing he'd be sure to have a 'dead-man's' watch I'd be able to afford.

When we arrived home I noticed that the clocks in both bedrooms were digital. They had built-in radios, snooze controls and switches that allowed you to wake up to the sound of a buzzer or an AM or FM radio station. When I asked Paul if he'd seen an old-fashioned, wind-up alarm clock with a bell on top, he looked as confused as the sales girl in Edments.

THE POEM

Watching

the change in the times
is recognised differently
   by my youngest son
& my eldest

the young fellow   year three
will tell me it's 9:15 or 10:42
   his brother   year ten
tells me it's quarter past nine
   or eighteen minutes to eleven

Darth Vader digitals replace Mickey
Mouse waving his hands in playgrounds
   & clockface classwork
is dropped for basic computing skills

poor kids only have a digital watch
   rich kids
can play Space Invaders on theirs
   or lap time dad's Porsche to school

no waking to jangling bells   our digits
wake to music   or get their first
buzz for the day   controlled of course
   by their AM/FM electronic digital
bedside companion   at 6:55
   or five to seven   depending.

Documentaries

BETWEEN THE LINES

Watching *(puns)*

the change in the times
is recognised differently
   by my *youngest* son   — *documentaries contain viewpoints*
  & my *eldest*

the young fellow   year three
will tell me it's 9:15 or 10:42
   his brother   year ten
tells me it's quarter past nine
     or eighteen minutes to eleven

some of these references will become out of date, but that's the point of the poem

Darth Vader digitals replace Mickey
Mouse waving his hands in playgrounds
  & clockface classwork
is dropped for basic computing skills

poor kids only have a digital watch
  rich kids
can play Space Invaders on theirs   — *documentaries contain information*
  or lap time dad's Porsche to school

no waking to jangling bells   our digits
wake to music   or get their first
a pun   buzz for the day   controlled of course   — *digits being numbers or children*
   by their AM/FM electronic digital
bedside companion   at 6:55
  or five to seven *depending.*

technological change provides choice; a concise summary

56

Documentaries

THE STING

This poem is built on 'differences' or 'opposites' between older and newer ways of knowing and telling the time: '9:15' versus 'quarter past nine', 'Darth Vader digitals' versus 'Mickey Mouse waving his hands', and so on. Find some more in the poem and make a list.

Now think about other sorts of changes that have taken place between your grandparents', parents' and your own generation. Did your grandparents or parents use pre-decimal currency – the penny, shilling and pound – and did they play 78 rpm records on wind-up gramophones? Look at the sorts of clothes they used to wear: fashion magazines and family photograph albums are excellent sources. Make a list of those that strike you as worth writing about, then use your list as the basis for a poem. I've referred to my poem as a 'documentary' because I use the first stanza to make a statement:

> 'the change in the times
> is recognised differently
>   by my youngest son
> & my eldest'

and the rest of the poem to explain the statement. You might like to start by writing something similar.

Using Language to Move Mountains

'THE MORNING SHUFFLE'

Words are action

THE TRIGGER

I've been an early riser most of my life. My sons have adopted many of my traits and habits, but not that one, especially not my eldest son, Mark. During 1985, when he was fifteen and beginning year eleven I found myself constantly devising tactical moves to get him up and on the move by seven to catch the train to school.

Through the school holidays it didn't bother me that he'd delay crawling out of bed much before one or two o'clock in the afternoon. I didn't even worry when he'd decide to have a big sleep-in and not jump up until four or five. We talked about it, of course, but he explained that this was his time, that he had no commitments and enjoyed the freedom of lying about and dreaming. Quite often when he'd rise he'd recount for his brothers and me his vivid experiences under the 'duna', maybe as a way of justifying what we all thought to be a waste of sun and light.

By the time school resumed in February the pattern had been set. It became increasingly difficult, as the weeks wore on, to get him mobile in the mornings. I could get him up by giving him a serve with the water-spray from the laundry, but it created a war that neither of us needed at seven in the morning. I knew I had to be more cunning and more subtle. I continued to give him more than a fair share of gentle reminders, but I really wanted him to be independent and self-reliant.

Initially when I'd wake Mark he'd respond by sitting up straight away, staring vacantly at me. And, for the first few weeks of the first term, he'd climb out of bed when I'd return to

Using Language to Move Mountains

THE TRIGGER

the kitchen. But when he became aware that I wasn't an ogre and that I wasn't going to beat him with his cricket bat, he became an opportunist, trying to sneak in an extra fifteen minutes or so of lighter sleep.

When this became regular, and the sounds of his feet dragging along the carpeted hallway were continually failing to eventuate, I'd have my first cup of coffee and stomp into his room, raising my voice to get him going. This would move him, all right. But he was soon yelling back at me. I'm sure that some mornings when he attacked his pillow he was visualising me. I didn't want to be cruel, but I didn't quite know how to be kind either. I'd return to the kitchen, feeling battered, but knowing that ten past seven was as late as we could possibly leave it if he was to get on that train. I started telling a few lies that I thought were okay under the circumstances. I'd do things like run into his room with a speedy voice and say, 'Quick, quick, get up, it's twenty past, jump up now ...' On one occasion, I yelled out that his girlfriend was on the phone. That got him up pronto, but he wasn't very amused.

Once up and in the shower he'd never want to get out. I finally schemed up a way that was foolproof, even though it would enrage him. I'd just keep turning the kitchen taps on and off, on and off, making the water in the shower so hot or so cold that he had to retreat. And when he did, it was usually with about three towels. He was a very tidy boy. Once the towels had been used, they could always be found spread over his bedroom floor from one side of the room to the other. I'd usually pick them up when I'd collect the coffee cup that was always left in his room, often untouched, with a thick, coagulated layer gripping the side of the cup.

I'd always drive him to the Adelaide Railway Station from our home in the west end of the city, most mornings with one eye on the road and the other on my watch, having to chance the amber lights and the ones that I'd refer to as 'pink'. When I did get home, relieved that we'd made it in time once again for the train, I was always busy trying to dream up another 'porky-pie'

Using Language to Move Mountains

THE TRIGGER

to get him moving tomorrow.

We had a rather firm discussion one night after school when I pointed out that I had an interstate reading tour coming up and that by then I expected him to be self-reliant. We eventually agreed that he should have dual alarm clocks, set five minutes apart. All this meant, however, was that I had to listen to the annoying sound of the two of them going off as he slept on. After a week of frayed tempers, we thought we'd found the answer. We got an old twenty litre kerosene drum, cut one end out and placed it alongside his pillow. We put both clocks inside. For the next few mornings I was doubly annoyed and felt no trace of guilt as I reverted to the water spray. But we talked some more, and this time I relented and allowed him to book Telecom early morning reminder calls. I left the phone to ring for as long as I could bear the sound, but it was never long enough to wake Sleeping Beauty. Even before the first semester ended I was resigned to the fact that I had to get him up each morning or enrol him in a night school. Soon after I'd accepted the five-day ritual of putting him on the shake, we had a house guest.

Komninos, a Melbourne poet, arrived for a week's work in schools and clubs around Adelaide, and we offered him the spare bed in Mark's room. I was still up when Komninos arrived home after his first night's work. We stayed up talking and draining coffee mugs until about three in the morning. When we realised that we were both as exhausted as our conversation had become, we decided to call it quits. But before heading off to bed Komninos asked if I had an alarm clock. He had to be on the road by nine. I told him that he was looking at one – and that I'd be in to put Mark on the shake at six forty-five without fail. I could see that he doubted me a little so I said, 'Komninos, five mornings a week I do the morning shuffle without fail. Just trust me and relax.'

He raised his eyebrows and said, 'You do the what?'

'The morning shuffle,' I replied.

'Mark is hopeless in the mornings. He'd never go to school if I didn't get him up, trust me.'

Using Language to Move Mountains

THE TRIGGER

Komninos stood there looking bewildered. 'The morning shuffle ... that's great!' His comment was not only a trigger but a challenge for me. Komninos went off to bed, laughing and murmuring softly the title of my next poem.

THE POEM

The Morning Shuffle

Hey it's 6:45   6:45
   time to get up my boy i say
gently gripping his ankle
   to rock him awake

it's time   c'mon   make a move
& he gives the sheet a twist
   screws himself up
one-eyeing me as i leave the room
   to wait
        & wait
            & wait
for the drag of tired feet
   & the kettle's slow boil

by 7:00   i'm full of beans
   forty-three
& jump into his room
   two octaves higher
GET UP   GET UP NOW
   & wrestle away his quilt

A W–R I G H T   I'M GETTIN' UP
he groans
   & strangles his pillow

THE SHOWER MY BOY   HIT THE SHOWER
   NOW
& i'm back for a second cup

at 7:10
   silence   makes me a liar

i fake *7:20*   & know
   Janine's on the phone
won't work   again

Using Language to Move Mountains

THE POEM

    & he shuffles   lead-footed over carpet
for a shower
    that could wash a family of six –
or seven
    till i hot/cold
        hot/cold
        hot/cold
the kitchen taps
    to receive his message
loud & clear

& when he's out
    the bedroom floor's re-carpeted
with towels
    while he drains a coffee mug
that's grown a skin

too late for eggs on toast
    the train won't wait

& three red lights are jumped
for the 7:50 express

but we make it   most times

& i drive home
    knowing
i'll be telling lies tomorrow

& i will.

Using Language to Move Mountains

THE CRAFT

In 'The Morning Shuffle' I (the poem's narrator) use different tricks of language (and action) to try to get my apparently immovable son on the go. First I speak to and act gently with him (first stanza). Then I become a little more insistent. By the third stanza I'm shouting, but it doesn't seem to work. So I resort to telling a lie. As in 'What Chance Has A Bloke Got', language in this poem is shown to be involved in a battle for power. I use language to try to 'move' my son according to my will and my perception of what's best for him. (But the 'password' that will allow me to impose my will on my son proves as difficult to find as the answer to the riddle of the sphinx.)

Think about other ways that language is used in power games between people.

_____ Using Language to Move Mountains _____

BETWEEN THE LINES

The Morning Shuffle

lower case italic letters denote a normal quiet voice tone

Hey it's 6:45   6:45
time to get up my boy i say
gently gripping his ankle
to rock him awake — *gently does it – or does it?*

it's time   c'mon   make a move
& he gives the sheet a twist
   screws himself up
one-eyeing me as i leave the room
   to wait
            & wait
                  & wait — *a spread of 'waits' indicates the length of time I am waiting – and for what?*
for the drag of tired feet
& the kettle's slow boil

by 7:00   i'm full of beans
   forty-three
& jump into his room — *the Nescafe advert '43 beans in every cup'*
   two octaves higher
GET UP   GET UP NOW
& wrestle away his quilt

upper case italic letters denote yelling or raising my voice

A W–R I G H T I'M GETTIN' UP
he groans
   & strangles his pillow — *is it really the pillow he is strangling?*
THE SHOWER MY BOY   HIT THE SHOWER
NOW
& i'm back for a second cup

at 7:10
   silence   makes me a liar
i fake 7:20   & know
   Janine's on the phone — *ten minutes later nothing seems to be happening – I begin to get devious*
won't work   again

_____ Using Language to Move Mountains _____

BETWEEN THE LINES

& he shuffles   lead-footed over carpet
for a shower
   that could wash a family of six –
or seven
   till i hot/cold ⎫
        hot/cold   ⎬ *the words dramatise*
        hot/cold   ⎭ *my actions*
the kitchen taps
   to receive his message
loud & clear

& when he's out   *sarcastic image*
   the bedroom floor's re-carpeted
with towels
   while he drains a coffee mug
that's grown a skin
                    I had 'formed' in an early
too late for eggs on toast *draft; this is stronger*
   the train won't wait

& three red lights are jumped
for the 7:50 express

but we make it   most times

& i drive home
   knowing
i'll be telling lies tomorrow

& i will.

Using Language to Move Mountains

THE STING

Getting out of bed for school in the morning is an act that most of us have had to go through, but we all do it in our own style. My eldest son mostly got out of bed with reluctance, my second son needed a nudge occasionally, but my youngest son generally had a shower and could be found tying a windsor knot in his school tie by the time I surfaced.

Write a poem about your early morning routine.

Using Language to Move Mountains

Rhythm, Rhyme and Sticks and Stones

'DON'T CALL ME LAD'

The sounds of words

THE TRIGGER

Shortly after Adelaide's Writers' Week one year I was moved to write 'Don't Call Me Lad' by a comment fired at me by my eldest son. Given that the trigger was expressed with a good deal of natural rhythm and emphasis, a voice pattern had formed that I couldn't ignore. The phrase kept echoing in my head.

I was sitting at the table in the dining room of the larger house we had moved into, typing a letter to a friend, when two of my sons slid open the glass doors that had been isolating me from the television program they'd been watching. When I looked up, I noticed an advertisement on the screen of the set and, sure enough, they'd come in to harass me.

Mark, the older of the two, stood right behind me. He was reading aloud to Shane who stood at the opposite end of the table, resting his hands on the edge and leaning in towards me, a smirk all over his face. When Mark finished reading, I screwed my head around and, being a proponent of free speech, told him politely to 'rack off' and go somewhere else to amuse himself and his brother.

I continued to tap the keys, but he took no notice of what I'd said. He started fidgeting with the top of my head, playing around where every strand of hair is a bonus. Without turning I flicked my hand back to swish him away, not taking my eyes off Shane, who was laughingly encouraging him. 'Go away,' I yelled, but the ads were still showing. They stood their ground. Mark started to harass me, in concert with Shane, banter flying from one end of the table to the other. They were saying things like, 'We'll get him a wig for Christmas'/'No, we'll get him a

THE TRIGGER

transplant'/'No, a hairpiece'/'What about if we can find some long strands and try to coil them?'/'No, that would never work, we'll get him a hat'/ 'No, a beanie', and so on. When the show on television started up again it was their cue to retreat. Instead of taking the short route back to the lounge, however, Mark walked around the table, allowing our eyes to meet. His parting comment was, 'I've got more hair on my balls than you've got, or had.' I threw my hands in the air in mock surrender and we all laughed. They went back to their TV show, closing the doors and shutting me off once again, but I was unable to shut that phrase out of my mind. The rhythm repeated itself and I jotted the words down, thinking even then that I had to use them. As it turned out, however, it wasn't just the words I used. I used the rhythm too.

A few weeks later I recognised that I could marry Mark's phrase with another, this one involving an incident with my sons after I introduced them as 'my three lads'. Then I remembered a scene in a prison with a member of my 'extended family' and how my use of the term 'lad' produced a negative reaction.

After some thought I decided that to make the poem authentic I needed to have an eighteen-year-old male as the narrator. I began to try to remember what it was like to be eighteen, attempting to make comparisons between eighteen-year-olds in my era and in the present. I remembered myself as an antagonist, and I see that trait mirrored in many young people today. I remembered thinking that I knew everything.

In November 1987 I married for the second time. I chose to have my eldest son Mark, then eighteen, as my best man. On the morning of the wedding my three sons and I went to the 'Flash Coffee Lounge' in Hindley Street, to meet a few mates who had come from interstate. My sons knew these blokes from their letters to me but hadn't met them personally. As my friends arrived I introduced them thus: 'Michael (etc.), I'd like you to meet my three lads, Mark, Shane and Paul.'

A couple of nights later I was winding my mind back over the events of the past few days when I became aware of my choice

THE TRIGGER

of words on that occasion. I started to think of the implications of the word 'lad'. I thought back to when I was eighteen and what my reaction to my own father calling me 'lad' might have been. Mark was eighteen. He wasn't a lad. Shane was sixteen, nearly seventeen. He wasn't really a lad either. Paul was only eleven: he most definitely was a lad. One out of three seemed poor odds for a man who used words to make a living. Why hadn't Mark or Shane challenged me on it? When I asked Mark, his reply was that he didn't want to cause a blue over it. Shane's reply came with a grin and a laugh. He said, 'If you call me lad again, old fella, I'll give you a Liverpool kiss.'

I made the same fatal error only a month later when conducting a writing workshop at Yatala Labour Prison. I had a mental block when I ran into Robert. I'd known him for over four years, but when he startled me by appearing in the room I couldn't place him. 'Orr, g'day, lad,' I said, 'how are y'.' My words went down like a rock in a sock from a great height.

When I wrote the poem I imagined 'Jim' coming home in the early hours of the morning, a few 'cones' inside him, and not really wanting to hear the old man going off his tree again. He anticipates his father's wrath and pre-empts it with his refrain, 'Don't call me lad', but then there is a hint of acceptance, or resolve, as the poem disappears off the page, with Jim whispering the refrain, 'I'm no longer a child'.

Rhythm, Rhyme and Sticks and Stones

THE DRAFT

No Longer (Jazz/Blues Beat)

Don't call me lad
     dad
just don't call me lad
got more hair on my balls dad
than y'v got –
    or had

i'm eighteen years old man
& i'll sink or i'll swim
just don't call me lad
     dad
my name – it's james
    or it's jim

& now that i can vote dad
my party is green
get away with those flags dad
red & blue are both mean

y' can roll up y'r shirt sleeves dad
& put on y'r tie
y' can curse & lay guilt trips
till yr black in the eye

but i can't find a job dad
year twelve was a waste
two friends have just died dad
too much of a taste

THE DRAFT

i'm mellowing out man
this home-grown is just wild
but don't call me lad
                dad
i'm no longer a child

so don't call me lad
                dad
i'm no longer a child.

THE POEM

Don't Call Me Lad

Don't call me lad
    dad
just don't call me lad
got more hair on my balls dad
than y'v got
    or had

i'm eighteen years old man
& i'll sink or i'll swim
just don't call me lad
    dad
my name is James
    or just Jim

& now that I vote dad
my party is green
get away with those flags dad
red & blue are both mean

y' can roll up y'r sleeves dad
& slip on y'r tie
y' can rant & lay guilt trips
but i'll spit in y'r eye

yeah i grow some plants dad
but i'm keeping it cool
four's not a plantation
i'm not such a fool

i just can't find a job dad
year twelve was a waste
two friends have just died dad
too much of a taste

THE POEM

yeah i get the dole dad
though it don't do much good
but don't call me lad
                        dad
i'd work if i could

now i'm mellowing out man
this home-grown is just wild
so don't call me lad
                        dad
i'm no longer a child

so don't call me lad
                        dad
i'm no longer a child.

I'm reminded when I look at the drafts of this poem that getting the rhythm just right was an important element. My second draft carries a note to myself that it's a 'jazz/blues beat' I'm looking for. My sons were into the music of George Thorogood and Jimmy Barnes when this poem was written. Our house resounded with bass sounds.

The opening lines of the first draft appear like this:

> 'Don't call me lad
> dad
> don't call me lad'

Looking at that first draft I see that I've snuck a 'just' in front of that third line. It's a quick 'just', not a well-enunciated one, more of a 'jus'. It sets the rhythm. Then I launch into the line fired at me by my eldest son: 'got more hair on my balls/than y've got/or had'. But I've added a 'dad' to it. I wanted to get that rhythm.

I probably read that first stanza aloud about a dozen times before I started writing any more of the poem because I wanted to hear and feel its rhythm.

My next line was 'i'm eighteen now man'. That's what I actually wrote down. But I knew the rhythm wasn't right. It quickly became 'i'm eighteen years old man' and I knew then I was finding it.

After writing 'i'll sink or i'll swim' I was snagged. I had to find a rhyme for 'swim'. My son's name is Mark, which wasn't going to work. I had to think about names and how they change. Robert becomes Bob. William becomes Bill. Michael becomes Mick. Ah yes, and James becomes Jim. But this isn't only a poem about my son, it's also a poem about the struggle to become an adult.

In the poem's first draft I wrote:

THE CRAFT

> '& now i can vote dad
> my party is green
> get away with your flags dad
> red & blue are both mean'

I soon changed the 'your' in the third line to 'those', because it seemed to distance itself from ownership. In a later draft I changed the first line to '& now that i vote dad'. This seemed to make the line more positive and the rhythm stronger.

On page two of my first draft I had written the words 'fierce/party animal/mellow out'. I would often hear those words used by my sons, nieces and their friends. Maybe I could sneak them into the poem. Poetry for me is about theft, or 'borrowing' people's language, or both. I saw a way to use 'mellow out' shortly afterwards. It became 'mellowing out' and I used it to start what was then the final stanza:

> 'i'm mellowing out man
> this smoke is just wild'

By draft two this had changed to:

> 'i'm mellowing out man
> & this smoke is just wild'

In draft three this became:

> 'i'm mellowing out man'

then:

> 'but i'm mellowing out man'

then:

> 'now i'm mellowing out man
> this home-grown is just wild'

and this is how those lines stayed through drafts four, five, six and seven.

———— Rhythm, Rhyme and Sticks and Stones ————

'Fierce' and 'party animal' never get used, but some things I'm happy to discard.

I thought about stories I'd been told by other teenagers and decided there was still plenty to say. I next wrote the stanza:

> *'y' can roll up y'r shirt sleeves dad*
> *& put on y'r tie'*

By draft four that had been simplified to:

> *'y' can roll up y'r sleeves dad*
> *& slip on y'r tie'*

That carried the rhythm better and I thought it caught neatly the motion of 'slipping' on a tie. The lines that followed started off in draft three as:

> *'y' can curse & lay guilt trips*
> *till y'r black in the eye'*

By draft four they became:

> *'y' can rant & lay guilt trips*
> *but i'll spit in y'r eye'*

'Rant' seemed a more natural word in young people's vocabulary than 'curse'. And the 'spitting in the eye' seemed to be a stronger way to show the family tensions and arguments I was being told about and involved in.

I started to think about those people I knew had been beaten by the system, who had succumbed to hard drugs and suicide. I used that knowledge to deliver the next stanza.

It was only the first line of this stanza that ever changed. It went from 'but i can't find a job dad' to '& i can't find a job dad' to 'i just can't find a job dad'. By draft five the stanza was under control. It had become direct and succinct.

I then thought I should put in a stanza about soft drugs before the one about hard drugs. During the writing of draft six I put in the stanza starting 'yeah i grow some plants dad' to precede the hard drug stanza. This stanza was without change. After looking

THE CRAFT

at the typed draft, I thought I had covered the topics that seemed to be the most talked about among the teenagers I had worked with and caught the rhythm of their language by using and recycling their language.

BETWEEN THE LINES

Don't Call Me Lad

                        Don't call me lad
a long pause ⟶   dad
                    just don't call me lad
spoken in a softer voice got more hair on my balls dad
                    than y'v got
a long pause ⟶   or had   *a quote from my eldest son*

                    i'm eighteen years old man
                    & i'll sink or i'll swim
                    just don't call me lad
                              dad
                    my name is James
                            or just Jim

                    & now that I vote dad
                    my party is green
                    get away with those flags dad
                    red & blue are both mean

                    y' can roll up y'r sleeves dad
                    & slip on y'r tie
                    y' can rant & lay guilt trips
                    but i'll spit in y'r eye

                    yeah i grow some plants dad
                    but i'm keeping it cool
                    four's not a plantation
                    i'm not such a fool

                    i just can't find a job dad
                    year twelve was a waste
                    two friends have just died dad
                    too much of a taste

Rhyme makes poems easier to follow and remember: it can make them funnier or more moving, but there's also a lot of repetition in this poem, and both the rhyme and the repetition are part of the rhythm

_____ **Rhythm, Rhyme and Sticks and Stones** _____

BETWEEN THE LINES

> *yeah i get the dole dad*
> *though it don't do much good*
> *but don't call me lad*
> > *dad*
>
> *i'd work if i could*
>
> *now i'm mellowing out man*
> *this home-grown is just wild*
> *so don't call me lad*
> > *dad*
>
> *i'm no longer a child*
>
> *so don't call me lad*
> > *dad*
>
> *i'm no longer a child.*

to explain the rhythm I've returned to the drafts: it's not easy to explain rhythm because it is intuitive

Rhythm, Rhyme and Sticks and Stones

THE STING

I want you to write a poem using the tools of rhyme and repetition. But I also want you to think about the 'names' people call each other (or themselves), and how these reflect social inequalities or skirmishes for power. In ancient times, poems were often written as 'social exchanges' between warring parties.

Maybe your parents insist on calling you by a nickname that was fine for you when you were at primary school but now makes you feel embarrassed or offends you. Here's your chance to let them know how you feel about it. Or try putting yourself in the shoes of someone who endures racist tags or taunts or suffers name-calling because of age or gender.

9 Portrait Poems

'POEM FOR ANNIE'

In poetry a portrait can include dialogue and narrative

THE POEM

Poem for Annie

In a space of twenty years
she's had three husbands
   three names
& three children to remember
two of them

& it's only in the past
five years
   they've worked out
who they are

but she knows about work –
   she's spent a lifetime
doing it
   typing endless words
(including these)
   or using others to answer
phones
   always too busy to check
the pedigrees
of those she stayed with
   & they've all turned out
mongrels
   that couldn't/wouldn't
work

they beat her badly in each deal
   or in the middle of the night
& she looked on while friends
got diamond rings
   & learned to hide when she got
black ones

THE POEM

    & then she met Brian
      poor
          poor
              mis-understood Brian
who needed a mother
    not a wife

but they never married
    she just lived with him –
till he jammed a glass
into her face
    smashed two teeth
& slashed her lower lip

but she's laid charges now –
    & that's a first

*but only because he showed
no remorse*
    was what she told me

& when her second son informed
her that he'd found him
    & smashed him in the face
with his motor-bike helmet
till he cried NO MORE
    she cried

*you'll never beat violence
with violence*

& it isn't just her hair that's
fair

Portrait Poems

THE POEM

but mum
 i warned him when he
blackened y' eye six months ago
 i told him i wasn't a kid
to tell a lie

her stitches came out yesterday
 & make-up will hide that
slightly visible scar

the deeper one she's been working on
with sedatives

& the crowns go on
in two weeks time
 so i can't call her *fang*

& i can only hope that then
 she'll never be crowned
again.

THE TRIGGER

This is the first poem I wrote about my elder sister. As much as this poem is for her, it is for all her sisters, those battered women, victims of domestic violence, who are spread across our nation. It was Annie who said after I published the poem that it was 'for all her sisters too'.

'Poem for Annie' is a poem that I wish I never had to write. But I had to do it to try to understand her situation and to try to come to terms with it. There's not much fun in hanging dirty washing on the line, but it's a fact that we live in a society that tolerates some forms of violence. If people don't speak up about domestic violence when they're aware that it's occurring, their passive acceptance gives more power to the perpetrators. There should be no room in our society for relationships based on violence and domination. Poetry mightn't be able to change the world, but it can become a medium to make people examine their values and attitudes.

After Annie read or heard me perform a poem about another family member, she'd often jokingly say, 'When are you going to write a poem about me? When will it be my turn?' And usually my laughing reply would be that she was too dull, too boring and uninteresting. We both knew this wasn't really true, but she'd always settle happily for it. As it was she waited five years.

It was early in 1988 when she last became a victim. The days were long and hot, the perfect climate for violence. She'd been a victim before: three times in three marriages. This time, however, the attack was horrific. I'd been given an inkling from one of my sons that something had occurred, but he didn't, or wouldn't, elaborate.

With my suspicions aroused I phoned Annie, but it was her teenage daughter who answered the phone. She told me that Annie wasn't in and began giving me vague answers. I explained to her that I felt something was wrong and convinced her that I knew more than I did. She told me that her mother didn't want me or my two brothers to become involved, that it was her concern and that she would deal with it on her terms. When I asked about the extent of her mother's injuries, she told me that

THE TRIGGER

I'd have to give her an undertaking first that I wouldn't interfere. She explained then that Annie had two teeth knocked out and a cut under her lip, which had been stitched. I was horrified, angry and sad at the same time, biting my own lip that I'd given such an undertaking and trying to comprehend how this bloke, with whom she had been living for a year, had been able to do such a thing. My niece went on to explain that her mother was 'safe' now, staying in a women's refuge, and then she began to ease away from me, promising to make sure that Annie returned my phone call. I asked her to ring her mother immediately, to tell her to jump into a cab and come to my home where I would pay the fare. I told her to let her mother know that she could stay with me indefinitely and that I'd speak to our brothers and seek their co-operation in allowing her to handle the situation as she best saw fit.

Annie arrived thirty minutes later, her face swollen and her mouth closed to contain the embarrassment of having two teeth missing. She spoke to me quietly with her lips barely parting. When we embraced there were tears and there were many more over the next eight weeks that we stayed together. But there was laughter too some days, especially after she overcame the initial fears of opening her mouth. Gradually she became more confident, even smiling sometimes. Soon the swelling began to subside and the stitches were removed.

Over the weeks that she stayed with me, she gave me quite a few triggers to write her poem. One of them was a phrase I heard her say to her son: 'You'll never beat violence with violence.' It's true, of course, but sometimes when we're wronged or when the people we love are wronged, our animal instincts urge us to pin the sheriff's badge on our chest and deal out our brand of rough justice. I know, and my brothers know it too. We've tried to settle our hurt that way before. This time, however, we stood back and offered Annie our support.

The activating trigger, the one that spurred me to begin the poem, occurred during the early hours of the morning when I was hard at work. It's my habit to read my work aloud when I'm

THE TRIGGER

drafting it and I often pad around the carpet while I do it. That's what I was doing when a glint in the carpet caught my eye. I knelt down and picked up a piece of crumpled silver-foil from the pile and put it in an ashtray. About an hour later, once again pacing the floor and reading, I found another piece on the opposite side of the room. Now my Virgo trait doesn't allow me to be so slack that I could have missed two pieces when I'd cleaned the room earlier. This time, I unwrapped the folded, crumpled ball of silver-foil and pressed it flat. Squinting under the table lamp, I read the brand name of a sedative stamped on the foil. I realised then that Annie must have discarded these two pieces earlier in the night, before I'd even started work. It began to play on my mind that she needed medication to sleep. I decided that I'd leave what I'd been working on and write a new piece based around her and her turmoil.

The poem begins with Annie's history: that she has had three different married names, has borne three children to two of those men, that with each marriage her children had adopted a different surname, only deciding during the last five years which of those names they would carry into their adult lives.

Annie has worked all her life through need, usually as a receptionist/typist or secretary. And with a busy work life and children's needs to be attended to, she's always busy. Too busy, I've suggested, to really consider the calibre of the men she married. As it has turned out, they were all either lazy or a combination of lazy, incompetent and unreliable.

Each of her three husbands abused her, often late at night when they returned home in a drunken state. While many of her girlfriends were given diamond rings and other jewellery, all she ever got was a series of black rings around her eyes.

After three unsuccessful marriages she met Brian. On the outside he seemed to be quiet and unassuming, lacking a bit of confidence, which didn't bother Annie. It was obvious he was insecure when he curled up in her arms like a baby, but he never appeared to be violent or dominating.

Late one night, after consuming a lot of alcohol, Brian

THE TRIGGER

thought he deserved more attention, got into an argument with Annie and thrust the glass he had been drinking from into her face, knocking out two teeth and lacerating her lip.

Even though she'd suffered many beatings during her previous marriages, Annie had never taken a spouse to court. This time, however, it was to be different. After returning home from hospital, her face stitched and swollen, she found Brian waiting in bed for her. She demanded that he leave the house immediately, but he refused, rolling on his side and away from her with a mumble that he wasn't going anywhere. She asked for an apology but was met with silence. She *demanded* an apology, but he just lay there, ignoring her pleas. It was then that she called the police to remove and charge him.

She asked her two adult sons and her three brothers not to seek Brian out and attack him. 'If anything happens to him it means that we've stooped to his level,' she said. A week later when her youngest son bragged about bashing him up, Annie was amazed and disappointed. She took the smile off her son's face with these words: 'You'll never beat violence with violence.' The line works in the poem because it is reported speech. It is not the poet's voice, but Annie's.

The poem continues to convey the narrative, advising that the stitches have come out and that make-up will hide the scar. But it isn't the visible scar that I'm thinking about. It's those pieces of silver foil. The really deep scar, the trauma that is carried after such an event, seldom fades.

One morning when I was working and her sedatives obviously weren't, Annie came in to ask if she could help me with some of my typing. It was about four in the morning and she must have been embarrassed as she entered the room, smiling nervously as she asked. 'Yeah, I wouldn't mind a break,' I said, 'Get into it, fang!' She looked a bit alarmed, maybe unsure that she'd heard me correctly and asked me to repeat my words. When I did she gave a nervous laugh and said, 'Is that the best you can do?' I looked her straight in the eyes and said, 'If we don't laugh about it, we might start crying ... and if we were to

THE TRIGGER

start, we might never stop.'

The poem ends with the wish that 'she'll never be crowned again.' That's my word play. But it's my hope too.

THE CRAFT

My poem for my sister began its life with the opening stanza:

> 'She's had three husbands now
>   three names
> & three children to remember
> two of them'

By adding as its first line, 'In a space of twenty years' and dropping the vaguer 'now', that is, by putting in a time-frame, I gave the reader a clearer picture of Annie's life (or the part of it I'm writing about). That small change made the poem more personally *for*, and more clearly *about*, Annie. In a portrait poem, small details can make all the difference.

I gradually expanded and changed the first few lines of the second stanza from:

> 'but she knows about work
>   she spent a lifetime
> typing endless words'

to:

> 'but she knows about work –
>   she's spent a lifetime
> doing it
>   typing endless words
> (including these)
>   or using others to answer
> phones'

The change from 'she' to 'she's' makes it clear that she's still busy working, 'typing endless words'. The bracketed line '(including these)' is almost like a personal 'thank you' to Annie. The last two lines show that she works as a receptionist as well as a typist, and build up a picture of a woman who is too busy (spending a lifetime working, typing endless words, even being asked by her brother and friends to type their words, answering phones) to pay proper attention to the sort of men she's involved with. In the lines that follow, the play on words with

THE CRAFT

'pedigrees' and 'mongrels', where I use terms normally applied to dogs to describe her men, is intentional.

In the fourth stanza, what I originally wrote as:

> '   & while her friends
> got diamond rings
>   she collected black ones'

I rewrote eventually as:

> '& she looked on while friends
> got diamond rings
>   & learned to hide when she got
> black ones'

Annie's 'looking on' to her friends' good fortune and 'learning to hide' her own misfortune from them adds a dimension to the poem that accurately reflects those aspects of her life that I'm writing about. It conveys a message to the reader about the loneliness often experienced by victims of domestic violence.

I made those changes to 'soften' the poem. But when I changed the fifth stanza from:

> '& then she met Brian
>   poor
>   poor
>   Brian'

to:

> '& then she met Brian
>   poor
>   poor
>   mis-understood Brian'

I made it 'harsher' by adding the sarcastic 'mis-understood'.

Portrait Poems

BETWEEN THE LINES

Poem for Annie

In a space of twenty years
she's had three husbands
   three names
& three children to remember
two of them

& it's only in the past
five years
   they've worked out
who they are

but she knows about work –
   she's spent a lifetime   *a play on the word*
doing it
   typing endless words
(including these)
   or using others to answer
phones
   always too busy to check
the pedigrees
of those she stayed with
   & they've all turned out
mongrels   *a hand of cards*
   that couldn't/wouldn't   *a hand in marriage*
work

they beat her badly in each deal
   or in the middle of the night
& she looked on while friends
got diamond rings
   & learned to hide when she got
black ones

around her eyes

Portrait Poems

BETWEEN THE LINES

inset words to slow the reading – for sarcasm

& then she met Brian
poor
    poor
        mis-understood Brian
who needed a mother

inset to emphasise the pause

not a wife

but they never married
  she just lived with him –
till he jammed a glass
into her face
  smashed two teeth
& slashed her lower lip   *criminal charges*

but she's laid charges now –
& that's a first

italics denote her words

*but only because he showed
no remorse*
was what she told me

& when her second son informed
her that he'd found him
  & smashed him in the face
with his motor-bike helmet   *raised voice*
till he cried NO MORE

italics denote her response

she cried   *double meaning to these two words: her voice cried out and she cried tears*

*you'll never beat violence
with violence*

100

& it isn't just her hair that's
fair

a pun

Portrait Poems

BETWEEN THE LINES

but mum
   i warned him when he
blackened y' eye six months ago
   i told him i wasn't a kid
to tell a lie

her stitches came out yesterday
   & make-up will hide that
slightly visible scar

the deeper one she's been working on
with sedatives *on her broken teeth*
& the crowns go on
in two weeks time
   so i can't call her *fang*

& i can only hope that then
   she'll never be crowned
again.

            a play on the word crown
            or crowned — as in being hit

Portrait Poems

THE STING

In 'Poem for Annie' I'm writing a 'portrait' poem of my sister and also writing about domestic violence. There's probably someone you know whose life is made difficult through some social injustice. Write down a list of some of the telling details by which you recognise a person's suffering. Remember small details are important in portrait poems.

Make a portrait poem from your list of observations.

10 Puns

'OVERTIME'

Puns rely on double, even triple, meanings

THE TRIGGER

Soon after I began work as poet-in-residence with the Amalgamated, Construction, Mining & Energy Union (CMEU) I recognised that some rivalry existed between that union and the Australian Building and Construction Workers Federation (ABCWF), formerly known as the Builders Labourers Federation (BLF). 'I'm a member of the BLs and proud of it' seemed to be the slogan of most rank-and-file members.

I recognised a reluctance on the part of some union members to accept my position as relevant and soon became aware of the political game-playing that goes on as part of daily life on the sites. During one building strike, I went to the site to talk to some members. I approached a group of twenty blokes sitting in Rundle Mall and said, 'G'day, I'm Geoff Goodfellow, the poet with the CMEU. I know you blokes are all BLs, but I'd like to find out what this strike is about so I can write a poem.' Three or four of them told me to 'go off' or something like that. With the exception of one bloke who assumed the role of speaker, the remainder gave me dark looks and moved along to sit on other benches. The speaker, who remained seated, made the point that they didn't want to talk to me or any other writer for that matter. He went on to say, 'The media are all right-wing dogs who never fail to misrepresent workers' views. The BLs don't talk to writers.'

I couldn't take the hint, though, and began to explain that I wasn't from the media and wasn't right-wing, that I was simply writing a book of poetry based on the lives of workers. I told him that I knew there was some friction between the two

THE TRIGGER

unions, but that, at the end of the day, all members go home with the same blisters and callouses, the same cuts and bruises, the same tiredness, and that I didn't give a damn whether a bloke was a tradesman or a labourer. I had one brother who was a carpenter, I said, and another who was a labourer, but I didn't use those categories to distinguish between them. 'The important thing,' I said, 'is that I get accurate information so I can publish a book that is true to life. I'm a worker too. It's just that I work with words.'

'We've been told not to talk to no one,' he said. He looked me square in the eyes and said, 'Can't you take a hint, mate?'

I was honest and told him that I couldn't and kept on pestering him, asking him personal questions about his reasons. Gradually I wore him down. He began to tell me things I already knew in a vague sort of way, but while he told it to me he kept repeating 'You'll get no information from me'.

The younger blokes working on sites are increasing their take-home pay by working overtime to meet their increased mortgage payments, he told me. He pointed towards the group of men who'd walked away from us and said, 'Look at 'em, mate, they're tired.'

Through our conversation the bloke pointed out that most of the men in that group had been recently divorced. It was the strain and the constant pressure that had been the main cause, or so he told me. He said they'd been arguing with their bosses constantly but had to accept defeat and 'cop it sweet', knowing that their mortgage payments and car payments and other expenses had to be met each week. They just didn't want any more overtime or shift-work. He told me that the workers didn't argue among themselves because they had to work alongside each other, day in and day out, and that a physical fight meant instant termination. The up-shot of that was that they'd been going home and 'blueing with the missus and kids', putting further stress on their marriages. When the marriage finally did fall apart, they'd finish up not only paying the house mortgage but a solicitor too. 'They can't win,' he said.

Puns

THE TRIGGER

The bosses were on their backs all the time, urging the completion of the job before the specified date on contracts to avoid having to pay a penalty clause. If a worker refused to work overtime, quite often the boss would be looking for an excuse to fire him, knowing that a big queue of eager workers was waiting for a start.

My main man explained that they'd called this strike to 'buy some time'. They needed to recuperate. Some of them weren't turning up each day because they were staying home trying to salvage their marriages. For most of them, he told me, 'it's just too late'.

What his story really spelt out to me was that, although we need to earn an adequate income, we need enough time in our lives to nurture our personal relationships. He wasn't a marriage guidance counsellor, a social scientist or a social worker, he was a builder's labourer and a good bloke.

Unwittingly he had given me a trigger, though perhaps not the one I'd gone looking for. I left him after about half an hour, excited by the prospect of finding a fresh way of telling people what they already knew.

THE POEM

Overtime

It's a hard earn on the tools
but y' don't see any young blokes
give a Saturday away he told me
   not now

these young blokes with mortgages
   they're fighting to survive

they need that extra day
   but even then they're beat

just look at 'em mate
   they're tired ...
y' can see it in their eyes
& in the drag of steel-capped boots
   fair dinkum –
they're fighting to survive

they're fighting with their bosses
& they're fighting with their wives
   & what the banks don't get
solicitors do

they're pressured all the time

the bosses want completion dates
to come in undertime
   & if they won't work overtime –
all the time
   it's an odds-on bet they won't
be working anytime

& all the time they're scheming
how to buy some time

but there is no time

they're paying for divorces now
   in overtime.

_____ Puns _____

THE CRAFT

I'd talked to a few building workers about their working lives and noted what I thought were key points. Referring to my notes I see that I've recorded:

'If the banks don't get it, solicitors do.'

'They're paying for divorces with their overtime.'

'They're fighting at work and fighting at home.'

'The ones that have the mortgages are fighting to survive.'

'They're tired, mate, y' can see it in their eyes.'

With phrases like those five, you might think that it was an easy task to write the poem. But it took me sixteen drafts. I wanted the poem to deal with complex issues in a simple but fresh and engaging way. The solution I came up with was the extended game-playing with the word and the notion 'time' from the fifth stanza to the end. My poem plays intellectual 'games' in its use of puns, but it works because the language is drawn from life. The speaking voice in the poem is always a building worker's.

Puns

BETWEEN THE LINES

Overtime

italics denote an actual voice – in this case, the voice of a building worker → It's a hard earn on the tools
but y' don't see any young blokes
give a Saturday away he told me ← *recycling language and phrases 'hard earn' 'on the tools'*
not now

knocking back the opportunity of working overtime – assists the reader to recognise that once it was common practice to say 'no' → these young blokes with mortgages
   they're fighting to survive

they need that extra day
   but even then they're beat

just look at 'em mate
   they're tired ...   ... *(create your own imagery)*
y' can see it in their eyes
& in the drag of steel-capped boots
fair dinkum – ← *a short pause*
they're fighting to survive

a pause for the reader to consider the two lines above → they're fighting with their bosses
& they're fighting with their wives
   & what the banks don't get
solicitors do

they're pressured all the time

the bosses want completion dates
to come in undertime
  & if they won't work overtime
long reading pause → all the time
   it's an odds-on bet they won't
be working anytime   ← *playing with the notion of time*
& all the time they're scheming
how to buy some time
beaten by the system → but there is no time

they're paying for divorces now
long pause → in overtime

_____ Puns _____

THE STING

I haven't specifically asked you to concentrate on the games that poets play with words, although I've mentioned puns, slang and other 'tricks of the trade'. The last five stanzas of 'Overtime' are *about* a social issue, but the stanzas gain their effectiveness through the extended game I play with the word 'time'.

Think of another word that crops up persistently among your friends. Play with that word by writing down familiar phrases in which it occurs. Write down synonyms (words that mean the same) or slang words commonly used in its place and think about ways in which the word can be used by different people to mean different things.

Make a poem out of your word games. Remember that your poem shouldn't *just* be a word game. It has to mean something to the reader and show something about the part of your world where you use the word.

Puns

Researching

'OLD WAYS/OLD DAYS'

*Researched poems musn't sound like
they've been researched*

THE TRIGGER

Within a month of taking up my residency with the CMEU I was approached by the arts officer from the United Trades & Labor Council of South Australia to write a poem on the terrazzo industry. They wanted a poem to complement an exhibition they were mounting, based on the history of terrazzo workers, to be launched during the Adelaide Festival of Arts. At the time the request reminded me of familiar days at Hampstead Primary School. Mrs Anderson would write a topic on the blackboard like 'A day at the beach with Grandma' and we were expected to reply with a full page of illuminating facts. Some of the kids I went to school with were very poor and often didn't have a grandma. I had half a mind to tell the arts officer this – or suggest that, if she were to order a pizza, she'd need to say what she wanted on top. Would she ask for anchovies and chilli or would it be pineapple and ham? Did she want something savoury or sweet? I thought if I did such a thing she might think me cheeky and antagonistic (Mrs Anderson always had). So I asked to talk to some former terrazzo workers. But, like Mrs Anderson, she had an excuse. She began to explain that many of them didn't speak English very well. I insisted that I'd need facts about their lives to be able to write anything of substance and kept probing. She had the oral histories of three of them and offered to let me use them. Later that same afternoon, thirteen typed pages arrived on my desk. Here were the lives of Marcello De Nicolo, Gino Di Giusto and Tino Dalle Nogare. Although I was pleased, the approach seemed impersonal. I would have liked to have heard their voices, felt their hand-shakes, got some sense

THE TRIGGER

of their size and presence. I tucked the transcripts into my black leather bag, unexcited by the prospect of reading them. I needed to meet the workers, or so I thought.

Later that evening, just before midnight, I climbed into bed, still wide awake and thinking that I should read something before turning the light off. The oral histories, I thought. That way I could go back to the arts officer to press for a personal meeting, arguing that the written accounts were too distant, too removed for me to get a feel for a poem.

What a suprise I got when I started to read them! After just a few lines I knew that I'd already met these men. Well, not these same men exactly, but men so similar that I had no trouble recognising the voices that were rising from the pages. As I raced through their stories I could see Vince and Sammy once again, two Italian blokes I'd worked with years ago. Both of them had been solid plasterers, among other things. We'd worked together for some time in the 1960s as a three-man team: I sprayed concrete into a hole in the ground and they screeded it and floated it off, turning our work into swimming pools. I was thinking that Vince and Sammy would know not only these men, but also their skills. I kept on reading, recognising similarities and noting the points to include in their poem. But all the time I was haunted by the echoed voices of Vince and Sammy, hearing again their broken English, the voices of new Australians, the one voice that would become the poem.

THE POEM

Old Ways/Old Days

*If you're talking terrazzo
   you're talking Italian
don't you worry about that*

*terrazzo
   as Italian as mortadella –
so beautiful you wish sometimes
you could eat it*

*but no one eats from it
today
   not from the labour anyway –
just from the table top
   yes   Alfresco in Rundle Street
they're got them
   & sometimes the feel & desire
lures me there to sip short black
   but always i think of the old days –
head down   bum up
   hand polishing till my fingers
bled
   no   men won't do that now*

*i always loved my art
   but like so many other men –
i kept my secrets*

*& now –
terrazzo to terracotta
   Trieste to Tranmere
that's the way things go*

_____ Researching _____

THE POEM

ah   the old days
*   jealous of my woman*
jealous of my job
*   both of them holding the eye*
like a Mona Lisa

now i go to bed with my
wife & aching back
*   dream of terrazzo –*
knowing that everything must change
*   everything has its price*
& only my work
*   can survive.*

THE CRAFT

Sometimes I tell people's stories through poetry by simply stealing the language that comes out of their mouths and recycling it on the page. Sometimes, however, I join their words with mine and marry the two. When I have the opportunity to speak face-to-face to a person, I'm likely to adopt the first strategy, especially if they are interesting and have something colourful to say. For this poem, I got most of my information from the thirteen pages of transcript.

One of the men who had worked in the terrazzo industry said he had worked 'head down, bum up'. Now I don't know too many Australian-born manual workers who would use language in that way. Most would say they had worked 'head down, arse up and into it'. This one phrase made me think about migrant workers and their different use of language. I soon began to feel the rhythm of the language that Italian migrant workers had used around me.

When writing the first three lines, I stood them apart and set them as a stanza or likely statement. They remained unchanged. In the second stanza I wrote:

> *'terrazzo*
> *as Italian as mortadella –*
> *and sometimes*
> *it just looks*
> *so beautiful*
> *you wish sometimes*
> *you could eat it'*

After looking at that I realised I had too much padding. I removed the third and fourth lines and presto! It worked. It still needed something though. I took the last three lines, linked them to become two lines and the rhythm and flow found themselves.

I drafted the second to last stanza this way:

THE CRAFT

> 'ah   the old days
> of Adelaide in the 50s
>   they feed me
> memories of beauty'

I knew I was close with these lines, but they said too much and yet not enough. That's a contradiction. The too much was the line 'Adelaide in the 50s', so I scrubbed it out. But the following lines don't *show* the beauty, they try to *tell* it.

I needed some imagery to convey it. I re-read one of the oral histories and recognised the protective nature of one of the participants towards both his girlfriend and his work. I thought I could convey that best this way:

> 'ah   the old days
>   jealous of my woman
> jealous of my job
>   both of them holding the eye'

But then I was stumped. Holding the eye like what? Like something or someone. Like Mona Lisa perhaps. Her portrait caught the imagination of the world and she was undeniably Italian. I found an image that almost everyone recognises and set myself up to slip out of the poem and off the page after the next stanza.

BETWEEN THE LINES

Old Ways/Old Days

If you're talking terrazzo
you're talking Italian
don't you worry about that

a long pause – let the   terrazzo
'terrazzo' word ring in   as Italian as mortadella –   *or/as Australian as a meat*
the ear   so beautiful you wish sometimes   *pie – or/vegemite – the*
   you could eat it   *dash at the end signifies*
     the reader to think about it

but no one eats from it
today
    not from the labour anyway –
just from the table top

pause 'yes' pause   yes   Alfresco in Rundle Street   *signifies reader to think*
they're got them   *about, if not from the*
& sometimes the feel & desire   *labour, what?*
lure me there to sip short black

pause or delay in reading   but always i think of the old days –
head down   bum up
pause   hand polishing till my fingers
bled

   no   men won't do that now   *not my work but my art!*
pause either side of the   *there appears to be no*
word to strengthen it   i always loved my art   *separation between the two*
but like so many other men –
i kept my secrets

short pause   & now –
terrazzo to terracotta
a long pause   Trieste to Tranmere   *dash signifies a pause to*
that's the way things go   *consider how many other*
     men/a few/most?

the direction of change, the
direction the workforce has
travelled

a certain acceptance
in the voice

Researching

BETWEEN THE LINES

ah *(pause)* the old days
   jealous of my woman
jealous of my job
   both of them holding the eye
like a Mona Lisa

   now i go to bed with my
   wife & aching back   *of being younger*
   dream of terrazzo –
pauses   knowing that everything must change
   everything has its price
   & only my work
   can survive.   *is that more than faith?*

Researching

THE STING

I was only able to write this poem after doing some research. I needed to find out more about the terrazzo industry and about the terrazzo workers' lives. The only materials available to me were oral history transcripts.

Try a bit of research yourself. You could, for example, interview someone in your community about their working life. Try to pick someone whose work you find interesting. Listen closely to what they have to say. You might be able to tape-record the conversation, but ask permission first. Focus on the 'telling phrases'. If you're not recording the conversation, write down as much of the conversation as you're able to remember. Use those parts that really 'display' the person's working life as the basis for a poem.

12 Satire

'POETRY IN THE WORKPLACE'

Satire means biting back

THE POEM

Poetry in the Workplace
for Lindsay Thompson, General Manager,
South Australian Chamber of Commerce & Industry

*They had their chance
to learn poetry at school* he said
   it's a bit late now

but Mister Thompson's
talking out of school
   his standards measured
by dollars
   not sense

from Enterprise House
on leafy Greenhill Road
   you can bet he'd be
well-versed
   he'd know the 100% write-off
for removing asbestos
from out-dated public buildings –
but as for blue asbestos claims
   it's a bit late now

& maybe Mister Thompson knows
a sonnet has just fourteen lines

but would Mister Thompson know
the weight of workers'
steel-capped boots
   or just that weight of coin
required to replace a pair?

THE POEM

& would Mister Thompson know
how families deal with death
when a scaffolder takes a dive?

would Mister Thompson then respond
to a union call for increased safety?

or would Mister Thompson simply say
   it's a bit late now.

THE TRIGGER

I was awarded a Community Writer's Fellowship by the Literature Board of the Australia Council for 1990. The newspapers recorded a few lines about it, but apart from that my project attracted little attention. For the first six months of the year I would be poet-in-residence with the CMEU to give lunchtime readings in factories and on building sites, then I would spend three months developing my own writing, and then I would work for three months with the South Australian Drug & Alcohol Services Council in clinics, detoxification units, prison drug units and a live-in therapeutic community.

Late in January invitations were sent out by the CMEU to representatives of the construction industry, labour officials, politicians and the media to attend the launching of the union's 1990 cultural program 'No Ticket No Start' at an 11 AM stopwork meeting on a large Adelaide building site. Suddenly my idea of poetry readings on the job for building workers was under attack. Newspapers around the country, national TV news and current affairs shows and radio programs were all giving it coverage. Why? Because Lindsay Thompson, General Manager, South Australian Chamber of Commerce and Industry, lambasted the project, labelling it 'sad' and 'pathetic', saying it would make Australia the laughing stock of the world. He went on to say, 'They had their chance to learn poetry at school. It's a bit late now.' Mister Thompson must have had a few busy days. The *Sydney Morning Herald* ran a page-three story entitled 'Boss can't see rhyme or reason for poems'. The *Age* in Melbourne put its story on page five with the headline 'Poetry and productivity do not rhyme, says SA employers' chief'. The *Australian*, in true contemporary spirit, ran the headline 'Construction bosses dread poet's society' and put its cartoonist to work. It's not often that a poet gets a national publicity campaign handed to him or her like that, but that's not all Mister Thompson did in his efforts to discredit my work. Members of building unions in four other states saw my performances on national television. What started out as a residency in South Australia soon extended to five states.

Satire

THE TRIGGER

The day before the official project launch, the Adelaide *News* said it was a 'War of Words'. That quotation proved to be the trigger for my poem. Part of my reason for taking poetry to building workers was to show them that language is power, that power isn't just physical.

When I began to structure the poem I used Mister Thompson's by then infamous remarks, 'They had their chance to learn poetry at school', and, 'It's a bit late now', to mock his stand.

THE CRAFT

This poem went through eight drafts, but the opening lines remained constant. Mr Thompson's words (the ones in italics) had been reported in the daily press around Australia. I figured that, if I was going to give him a verbal bagging, at least I should report his words faithfully. By turning his 'one-liner' into three lines, adding myself-as-reporter with 'he said' to the second line and applying my tap/tap/tap on the space bar, I fired some poetic rhythm into his comment.

In the second stanza I originally had:

> 'but it seems his standards
> are only measured in terms
> of dollars & cents'

which is very 'flat'. There's no magic in it. Compare that with the published version:

> '   his standards measured
> by dollars
>   not sense'

That is more concise. The spacing/pausing adds rhythm and meaning. The pun on 'dollars/sense' is more provocative and evocative than the bland 'dollars & cents' of the original. When I'm writing a political poem, I'm aware that it's my job to 'engage' my audience with playful use of language.

There are other poetic devices in the poem that I've used both to keep the reader interested and to give Mr Thompson a bit of what he's dished out. You might think about:

- why I choose to call him *Mister* Thompson throughout the poem, rather than 'Lindsay Thompson' or just 'Lindsay';

- how I turn back on him his line 'it's a bit late now' by repeating it in different contexts and how this is designed to provoke a questioning attitude in the reader;

THE CRAFT

- ☞ the clash between what I say Mr Thompson knows about (in stanzas three and four) and what I ask him in stanzas five, six and seven;

- ☞ how I use the tactic of repeated questions in those stanzas (five, six and seven) to build the poem to a crescendo; and

- ☞ how particular words and phrases including 'leafy', 'you can bet', 'talking out of school' and 'weight of coin' add to the poem's satiric tone.

BETWEEN THE LINES

Poetry in the Workplace
for Lindsay Thompson, General Manager,
South Australian Chamber of Commerce & Industry

*They had their chance
to learn poetry at school* he said
it's a bit late now

but Mister Thompson's
talking out of school
   his standards measured
by dollars
   not sense ← *or cents?*

from Enterprise House
on leafy Greenhill Road
poetic term and ↘ you can bet he'd be
common language well-versed
   he'd know the 100% write-off   *the dash signifies a short*
   for removing asbestos   *pause to absorb the facts*
   from out-dated public buildings –
a longer pause here to but as for blue asbestos claims
allow the above line → it's a bit late now
to impact

& maybe Mister Thompson knows
a sonnet has just fourteen lines ← *a poetic fact*

but would Mister Thompson know ← *know what?*
a long pause to consider the weight of workers'
how heavy those boots steel-capped boots
might be ————→ or just that weight of coin
required to replace a pair?

Satire

BETWEEN THE LINES

& would Mister Thompson know   *know what?*
how families deal with death   *families of whom?*
when a scaffolder takes a dive?

would Mister Thompson then respond
to a union call for increased safety?

or would Mister Thompson simply say
   it's a bit late now.

a long pause – before the hammer falls

THE STING

I bet there's someone you know – a fellow student, a teacher, someone you work with, a friend – who has made some important statement that has really got up your nose. Retaliate by writing a satirical poem. The secret is to take the original statement and twist and turn it.

With 'Poetry in the Workplace' we've gone from where we started in 'Beware of the Penguins' – in school – to the working world. Mr Thompson thinks that the proper place for poetry is in school, that it doesn't have any real relevance in ordinary working life. What do you think? You might want to write your response as an essay, a story, a poem, or a letter to the editor of a newspaper.

WAKEFIELD PRESS

Geoff Goodfellow's Poetry Trifecta

NO TICKET NO START

'These are powerful, abrasive, compassionate poems that give building workers an authentic voice not heard so clearly since the Green Ban days.'
Caroline Jones, *ABC Radio*
The Search for Meaning

ISBN 1 86254 264 3   RRP $5.95

RECOMMENDED RESOURCE FOR SACE AUSTRALIAN STUDIES
RECOMMENDED RESOURCE FOR SACE AND VCE WORK EDUCATION COURSES

NO COLLARS NO CUFFS

'This is poetry that means business…Goodfellow is proof that people will buy poetry, and will laugh and cry and ask for more.'
Kevin Brophy, *Australian Book Review*

ISBN 0 949363 07 3   RRP $9.95

RECOMMENDED RESOURCE FOR SACE AUSTRALIAN STUDIES

BOW TIE & TAILS

'Geoff Goodfellow…pushes poetry as something real, living, using the language of the heart and the street, the voice of battlers and the beaten, those who make it by the skin of their teeth, and those who don't.'
Carol Treloar, *The Advertiser*

ISBN 0 86254 996 6   RRP $12.95

RECOMMENDED RESOURCE FOR SACE AUSTRALIAN STUDIES

WAKEFIELD PRESS

Poetry

Across the Gulf   *J. Dally, A. Kipping and M. Lenore*
Algebra   *Steve Evans*
Bow Tie & Tails   *Geoff Goodfellow*
Edison Doesn't Invent the Car   *Steve Evans*
Friendly Street Poetry Readers
Inside Out   *Syd Harrex*
Monster Love   *Jeri Kroll*
No Collars No Cuffs   *Geoff Goodfellow*
No Ticket No Start   *Geoff Goodfellow*
Rites of Arrival   *Jeff Guess*
Satura   *John Bray*
Selected Poems   *Graham Rowlands*
Seventy Seven   *John Bray*
The Bay of Salamis   *John Bray*
The Bitumen Rhino   *Neil Paech*
The Inner Courtyard   *ed. Anne Brewster and Jeff Guess*
Three's Company   *D. McCulloch, D. McSkimming and E. Ward*
Under the Pepper Trees   *ed. Marcie Muir*
Walking to Bethongabel   *Robert Clarke*

WAKEFIELD PRESS

SOMEONE YOU KNOW
Maria Pallotta-Chiarolli

Someone You Know is Maria Pallotta-Chiarolli's biography of Jon, who is living with AIDS, and the story of their extraordinary friendship.

'I have rarely been so moved by a piece of writing, in a book or on stage or screen, as I was by the end of part five of *Someone You Know*.'
Robyn Arianrhod, *The Age*

'This book covers the issues that AIDS makes us confront and will help everyone involved in AIDS education.'
Ita Buttrose, Chairperson, AIDS Trust of Australia

ISBN 1 86254 271 6   RRP $14.95

WAKEFIELD PRESS

SELECTED POEMS
Graham Rowlands

Over the last twenty years Graham Rowlands has
gained a reputation as a one-man poetry industry.
There have been weeks when the pages of literally
any newspaper or journal in the country – from the
Australian to the *Egglayers' Gazette* – could be opened
and a Rowlands poem discovered.

'His poetry is intense, bare and often discordant.
Its mood can be brutal, ironic, disturbed, clever.
At the centre of a world of which he is both critical
and despairing is a highly perceptive intellect.'
                               Carol Treloar, *The Advertiser*

ISBN 1 86254 275 9   RRP $12.95

WAKEFIELD PRESS

MAGPIE
Peter Goldsworthy and Brian Matthews

This novel by two of Australia's leading writers is part argument, part collaboration and always irreverent fun.

'An exuberant comedy...The post-Dawkins world of tertiary education has never been so heartily and unrancorously lampooned.'
Peter Pierce, *Sydney Morning Herald*

'...a novel that dive-bombs current literary theory and rips hairs from academic and literary sacred cows.'
Katharine England, *The Advertiser*

'...a deftly composed, glistening assembly...*Magpie's jeu d'esprit* is a reminder of the pleasures of the text.'
Peter Hutchings, *Adelaide Review*

ISBN 1 86254 272 4   RRP $12.95